Stingrays

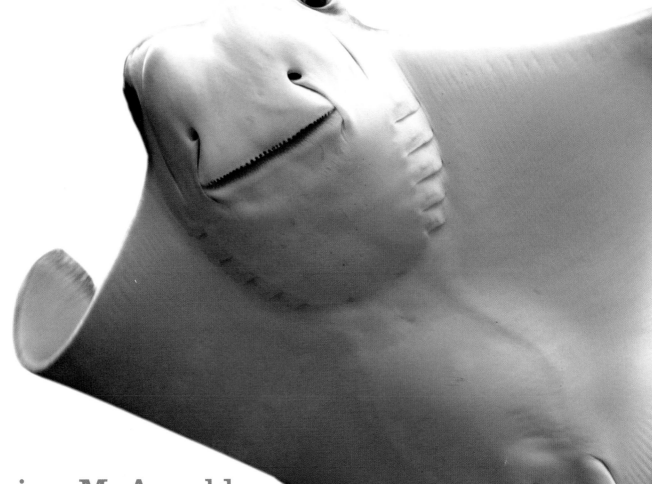

Quinn M. Arnold

CREATIVE EDUCATION • CREATIVE PAPERBACKS

seedlings

Published by Creative Education and Creative Paperbacks
P.O. Box 227, Mankato, Minnesota 56002
Creative Education and Creative Paperbacks
are imprints of The Creative Company
www.thecreativecompany.us

Design by Ellen Huber; production by Joe Kahnke
Art direction by Rita Marshall
Printed in the United States of America

Photographs by Alamy (Steffen Binke, David Fleetham,
Gaertner, imageBROKER, Jeff Rotman), Dreamstime (Kokhan,
Worapat Maitriwong, Olgavisavi, Kiryl Paddubski, Ian Scott,
Stephankerkhofs), Getty Images (Steven Trainoff Ph.D.),
iStockphoto (bthompso2001), National Geographic Creative (DAVID
DOUBILET, JOEL SARTORE/NATIONAL GEOGRAPHIC PHOTO
ARK), Shutterstock (Konoka Amane, Rui Manuel Teles Gomes,
Yann hubert, junyanjiang, photosthai), SuperStock (Michele
Westmorland)

Library of Congress Cataloging-in-Publication Data
Arnold, Quinn M.
Stingrays / Quinn M. Arnold.
p. cm. — (Seedlings)
Includes bibliographical references and index.
Summary: A kindergarten-level introduction to stingrays,
covering their growth process, behaviors, the waters they call
home, and such defining features as their long, thin tails.
ISBN 978-1-60818-782-9 (hardcover)
ISBN 978-1-62832-402-0 (pbk)
ISBN 978-1-56660-836-7 (eBook)
This title has been submitted for
CIP processing under LCCN 2016937127.

CCSS: RI.K.1, 2, 3, 4, 5, 6, 7;
RI.1.1, 2, 3, 4, 5, 6, 7; RF.K.1, 3; RF.1.1

First Edition HC 9 8 7 6 5 4 3 2 1
First Edition PBK 9 8 7 6 5 4 3 2 1

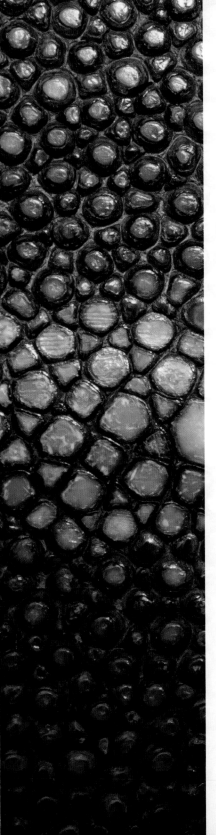

TABLE OF CONTENTS

Hello, stingrays!

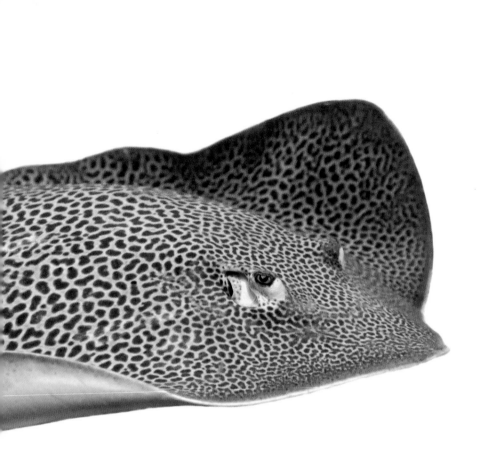

Stingrays are flat
fish. They swim in
warm waters.

Most live in oceans.

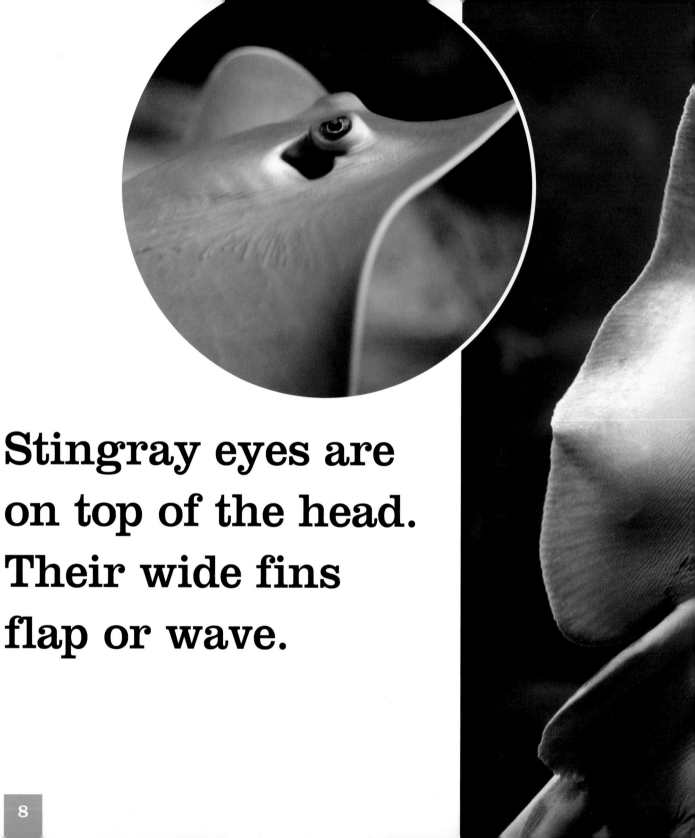

Stingray eyes are on top of the head. Their wide fins flap or wave.

9

A stingray's tail is long and thin.

It has a sharp spine.
The spine helps keep
the fish safe.

Stingrays eat
shrimp, clams,
and crabs.
Sometimes they
eat sea worms.

Their mouth is on the bottom of the body.

13

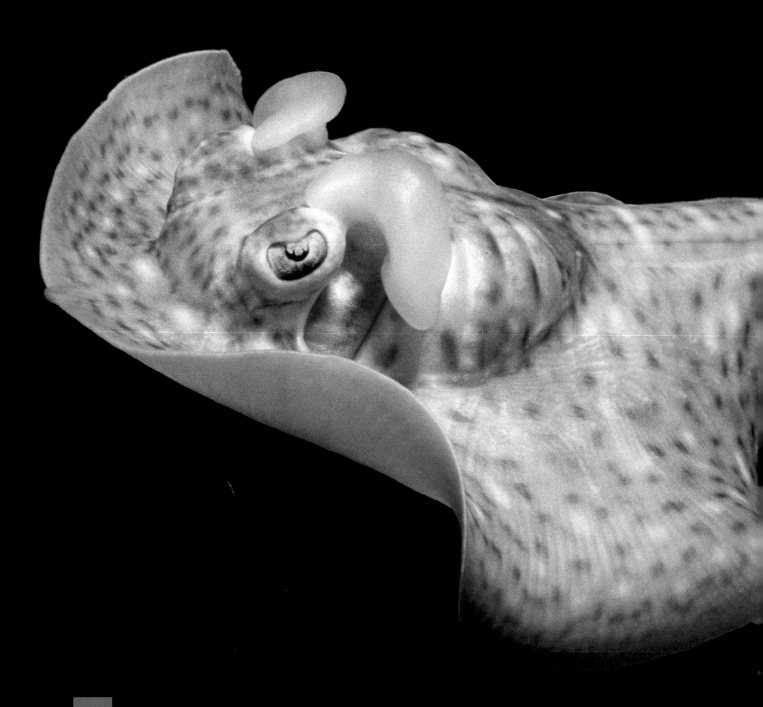

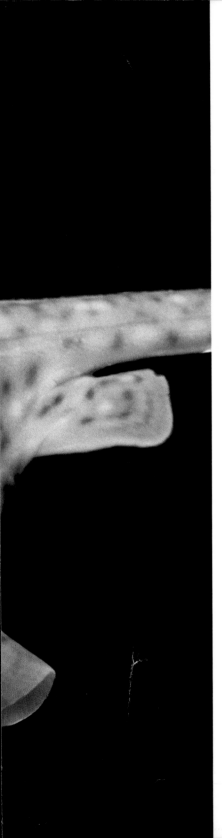

A baby stingray is called a pup. Pups stay in shallow water until they are bigger.

Stingrays hide in the sand.

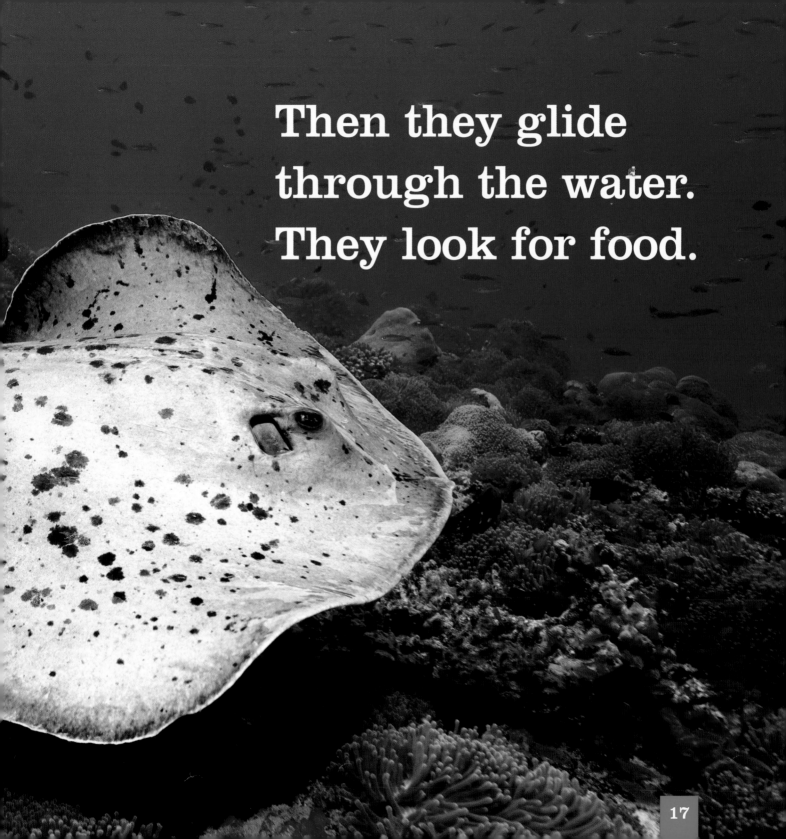

Then they glide through the water. They look for food.

Goodbye, stingrays!

Picture a Stingray

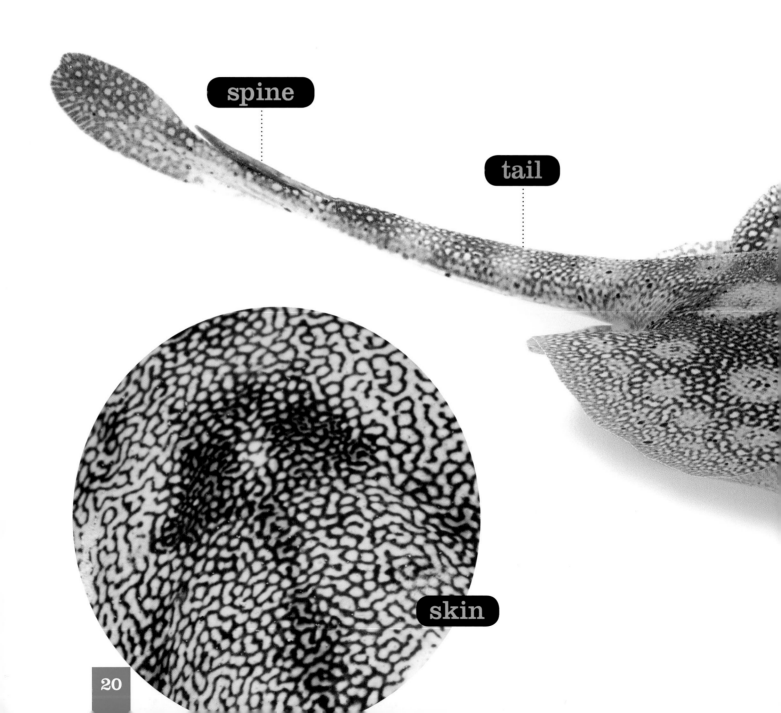

spine

tail

skin

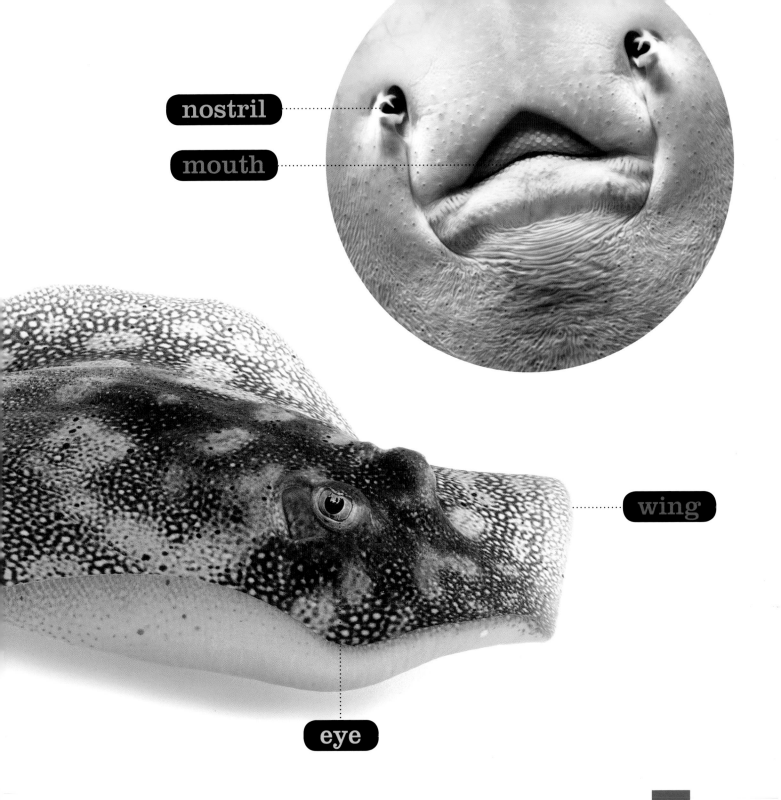

nostril

mouth

wing

eye

oceans: big areas of deep, salty water

shallow: not deep

spine: the hard, sharp part of a stingray's tail

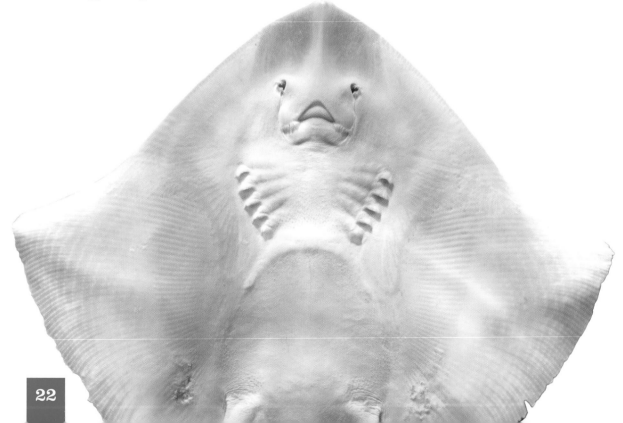

Read More

Raum, Elizabeth. *Stingrays.*
Mankato, Minn.: Amicus, 2016.

Rustad, Martha E. H. *Stingrays.*
Minneapolis: Bellwether Media, 2007.

Websites

Bluespotted Stingray Coloring Page
http://www.thecolor.com/Coloring/Blue-Spotted-Stingray.aspx
Color a bluespotted stingray using the online coloring tool.

How to Fold an Origami Stingray
https://www.youtube.com/watch?v=6gZirMi42N4
Make your own origami stingray.

Index